Baby Sleep Solutions

Exhausted? How to Get Your Baby Sleeping Through the Night in 6 Easy Steps

By: Katrina Villegas

Baby Sleep Solutions

This book is dedicated to my amazing family.

Joe, you have supported me through all of my parenting ideas and projects (like this book). Caroline and William, you fuel my passion and make this journey as a mom so rewarding. April Rey, I know you are always with us. You've helped me to realize that my writing matters.

Thank you all so much for being the best family I could have ever asked for.

Baby Sleep Solutions

Forward

Good sleep habits are so important to teach our babies. Just like everything else, we actually have to *teach* our babies how to have good eating and sleeping habits. These habits can be taught from birth. But not to worry, if you are a little late to the game with an older baby, it's ok. These healthy habits can be taught at any time, and you will be able to transform your baby's sleep habits. It is very doable with this realistic approach.

Teaching good eating and sleeping habits to your baby enables you, as a whole family, to prioritize sleep. With teaching these habits, your baby will learn to sleep through the night and, as a result, will be well rested and ready to learn and take on the world. The rest of the family will have uninterrupted sleep as well, and all will be well on their way back to being well rested.

There's no doubt that, in the early weeks and months, babies need to wake in the middle of the night. They simply can't go very long without needing to be fed. Their little bellies only hold so much food, so they need small quantities around the clock. If we can fill their bellies and teach them when to sleep, however, they can maximize their feedings and sleep longer stretches.

So, whether you are pregnant and planning ahead, have a newborn, or have a 10-month-old baby, this book is for you. You can successfully prioritize sleep to have your baby snoozing a full 12 hours at night.

In this book, I will describe EXACTLY what my husband and I have done to get our babies sleeping through the night by the time they were 4 months old. It truly is never too late to put these methods into practice. With these 6 realistic and easy steps, you can have your baby sleeping through the night as well!

So, Here's the Bad News —

There's no magical solution. You can't just snap your fingers and make this work.

You have to put a bunch of ideas together, figure out what works for your baby, and then work hard at it.

But Here's the Good News —

I'm going to outline the steps in this book for you, and all you have to do is implement! If you put these steps into practice, you WILL be successful in getting your baby to sleep through the night.

And Here's the Trick to Doing This —

Don't focus your energy on nighttime sleep!

I know, I know—you're sitting here saying, "But the goal is nighttime sleep!"

YES, but that is the last place you need to focus your efforts with your baby in the beginning.

First, you actually have to focus on the daytime with your baby. Once your baby has the daytime down, you will all be set up for success at night.

Data & Proof That This Works!

I once saw a meme floating around on Facebook that said, "Normalize Night Feeding," and proceeded to share a statistic (not sure where they got this) that 80% of 6–18-month-olds wake one to three times a night to feed.

I cringed when I read this.

It doesn't have to be this way! And we don't have to just accept that babies wake up all night long. If we help our babies and teach them (as we do with everything else), they can and will sleep at night.

First of all, who knows where that data came from, and second of all, it doesn't tell us anything. It simply takes the burden and stress off of parents to help their child sleep through the night by implying that it is "normal."

We don't know if those parents were feeding on demand, on a schedule, having supply issues, and on and on and on. And so, the data is meaningless.

I want my baby to sleep 12 hours at night in order to be healthy and happy—that all starts with a good sleep foundation. I also want to sleep well myself so that I am the best mom I can be.

So, here's the data I collected. I polled a group of parents that I know all share the same parenting strategies. We all feed our babies on a schedule, use eat, wake, sleep cycles, and use many of the tactics that I've outlined in this book.

I also know that no one did any form of "cry it out." I specified that I was excluding that data just to gain a glimpse of the impact of the basic tactics outlined in this book.

Keep in mind, this was an informal poll where parents self-reported their data. These parents definitely used schedules and eat, wake, sleep cycles. They may have also used the other tactics outlined in this book.

I don't know everything about each unique vote. I don't know if anyone had supply issues or if babies were premature, had tongue or lip ties, etc.

But the Data Speaks for Itself...

300 people participated in this informal poll. The following data represents when they had their babies sleeping through the night (a full 12 hours) using no form of cry it out.

80.4% of babies were sleeping through the night before 6 months of age!

Let That Sink In.

If you put these techniques into practice, your baby is most likely going to follow the 80% of other babies and be consistently sleeping through the night sometime during the first 6 months.

And It Gets Better.

76.5% were sleeping through the night before 5 months of age.

60.9% were sleeping through the night before 4 months of age.

And you might be the 23.4% that have your baby sleeping through the night before 3 months!

3.9% of babies were doing it in their first month. Rare, but possible.

18% of the babies weren't sleeping through the night until somewhere between 6 and 12 months of age.

And, only 1.6% of the babies were not yet sleeping through the night by 12 months.

I often have people tell me that I'm so lucky to have such good sleepers. I just smile and agree most times as it's a lot to explain.

But the Reality?

My husband and I work hard to get our babies on the right track and set them up for success. There's no luck involved.

We teach our babies how to sleep well.

We teach them how to put themselves to sleep.

We decide when it's time for our babies to sleep. Why? Because we, as parents, know best.

And so, we decide.

We work hard to find the right schedule. We put the work in for our babies, and it pays off.

Luck? No.

Hard work? Absolutely!

Doable? Yes! Like anything, you must put in the work. But it is achievable and, once you get the hang of it, easy to do!

What to Expect in This Book

One of the things I hate about parenting books, especially now that I am a mom with limited time, is the wasted space and fluff. I find myself skimming to the truly helpful parts and feeling like 60% of the book was a waste of my energy and merely the "philosophy" behind it all, rather than the "how to." When we are looking for parenting help, the parenting philosophies are interesting and all, but it's not the helpful part.

This book is going to cut all of that out—I promise you! I am a former chemistry teacher and engineer, which means I like concise, to-the-point writing that won't waste anyone's time.

So, with that said, let's get into the "How To" and get your baby sleeping through the night!

Table of Contents

These are the 6 steps you can start today, to help your baby prioritize sleep and start sleeping through the night. This guide is broken down into doable, realistic steps that are easy to implement. This is exactly what my husband and I did with our babies.

APPENDIX

Chapter 1

*Show Your Baby the Difference
Between
Day & Night*

One of the first things you should do with your newborn is help them to learn the difference between day and night. Your baby just spent 9 months inside of a dark womb. No standard has yet been set that he/she is supposed to be up during the day and asleep at night.

It becomes your job to teach your baby the difference!

When pregnant, many moms will notice that their baby is more active at night and is still during the day. Babies are lulled to sleep by the movements that a mother makes during the day. When at rest, however, babies seem to get a burst of energy and stay up all night long kicking. As a result, many babies have their days and nights confused.

Your first job as a parent is to teach your baby the difference between day and night.

How Do You Establish Day from Night?

Start your day at a consistent time.

We used 6 a.m. as our desired wake time. You can choose what works for you. Wake your baby up at this time to get ready for the day! Keep it consistent every day.

Light.

Open the curtains for natural light, and turn the lights on during the day.

Play.

Show your baby that it is time to be awake! Play, read, sing, etc.

Have a schedule throughout the day.

For newborns, you want to feed them every 2–3 hours. I'll outline specific schedules by age in Chapter 5.

Wake your child during the day. Get those feedings in, and don't let sleep go too long. Wake your baby after a nap to stay on schedule and set him/her up for success.

There's only so much sleep that a baby needs in a 24-hour period. You want to make sure you get your baby set up for a 12-hour nighttime stretch and plan the correct amount of sleep during the day. Do this by taking a look at the schedule chapter.

Darkness.

At nighttime, keep it dark. Use nightlights or small lamps, if you need them, to help you see well enough to feed your baby, etc. Limit light as much as possible, however. Use room darkening shades to help in the early evening hours.

Quiet.

At nighttime, keep it quiet. Whisper. Night is a time for sleep. You need to teach this to your baby.

Do not wake your child at night.

Unless you've been instructed to do so by your doctor, do not wake your child at night. Let your baby wake naturally for nighttime feedings.

Both of our children were born early (37 weeks and 34 weeks). As a result, we were waking them around the clock for a few weeks to make sure they received the nutrition necessary to get back to their birth weights. We still did all of the above steps to differentiate day feedings and nighttime feedings and were well on our way to establishing the difference of day and night.

Chapter 2

Get Your Baby Taking Full Feedings

The next thing to focus on is full feedings. If you get in the correct number of feedings during the day, but they are inefficient feedings, your baby is still going to be hungry.

Your baby might sleep for a few minutes and then wake up hungry and upset because he/she did not get enough to eat. Your baby will be snacking all day long as a result.

To prevent this, you want to encourage full feedings. Full feedings will ensure that your baby is getting good daytime sleep and enough food to, in turn, promote better, longer stretches at night.

So, full feedings are an essential thing to teach from the beginning.

Newborn babies love to fall asleep, especially when they are eating. Eating and the simple act of sucking puts them to sleep. This is why we give babies pacifiers to help them sleep. One of the biggest challenges in the early days is keeping your baby awake.

It is so important to keep your baby awake, however. An alert baby will finish eating and get a full feed. This means your baby will nap better, sleep better at night *and* your baby will learn to separate feeding and sleeping, which is HUGE. I'll discuss this further in Chapter 4 when discussing the purpose of the eat, wake, sleep cycle.

Tips to Encourage Full Feedings

Keep your baby awake.

Easier said than done in the first couple of weeks, but do what you need to do...

Keep the lights on.

Never try to feed your baby during the day with the lights off or when things are too comfy and cozy. Get the lights on and keep your baby stimulated.

Make noises.

Talk to your baby, have the radio on, read a book while your baby eats, sing a song—keep interacting so that your baby knows it's time to stay awake. This is for newborns and the first few months. Now, once your baby is easily distracted (around month 4) and looking and grabbing at things, you want to stay quiet and let him/her focus. At that point, find a quiet place with as few distractions as possible.

Tickle your baby's toes.

Sometimes your baby just needs some extra stimulation to stay awake.

Blow on your baby's face.

Those eyelids are closing, so this is exactly where they need some attention. Blowing on your baby's face will rouse him/her gently, and your child will likely open their eyes.

Put a wet washcloth on your baby's forehead.

A wet washcloth is usually my go to. I would keep one nearby when I was breastfeeding in the early days. When everything else failed to keep my babies awake, this tactic usually did the trick. It startled them just enough to wake up and keep eating.

Do a diaper change midway.

If your baby is being breastfed, have him/her feed on one side, then do a diaper change followed by feeding on the other side. For bottles, start the bottle and, when your baby loses interest, do a diaper change, then offer the bottle again.

A Note About Full Feedings

I used to think that a hungry baby wouldn't sleep, that a hungry baby would be upset. A hungry baby will let you know, right!? We saw firsthand with our son just how wrong that was. Typically, yes, a hungry baby is not going to sleep well and is going to let you know that more food is needed. *But there's always the exception. Our son was that exception…*

With our daughter, breastfeeding went pretty perfectly. I had raw nipples for the first two weeks and could hardly wear a shirt, and when she was around 4 months old, she started biting down. I called her my little shark. Luckily, she didn't have any teeth until she was 12 months old (and done with breastfeeding). But, for the most part, things went well. My supply was great and was strengthened by the schedules and routines that we put into place. She had a beautiful growth chart and was a nice chunky, healthy baby. All in all it was a blissful breastfeeding relationship.

When our son came along, things seemed to go just as smoothly. My milk came in fine. He was a NICU baby, so during the first week, I was pumping around the clock and bringing the milk to him to keep my supply up. The NICU had him on a 3-hour schedule. They'd give breast milk when they had it and formula the rest of the time. I'd try to breastfeed him while I was there visiting him for feedings. He latched and seemed to do pretty well.

It was a rocky start because he'd get so sleepy trying to feed and was exhausted by the time we were done breastfeeding. After the first couple of weeks at home, however, we had a great rhythm going. After each attempt at breastfeeding, we were supplementing with bottles to make sure he gained enough weight. We also woke him around the clock (yes even at night) for the first month, just to make sure he had a good start.

Eventually, he stopped taking the bottle. So, we just naturally assumed that he was getting enough food through breastfeeding and stopped the bottles. Our doctor agreed that, at that point, it was fine. He was eating and sleeping well. Everything seemed perfect. He was even sleeping through the night for 12 hours.

Well, at his 4-month appointment, he hadn't gained much weight since month 2. It was concerning. I was shocked because of how well he was doing with naps, nighttime, and seemingly the act of breastfeeding itself. His latch was good. All seemed *good*.

The doctor suggested that we add in more feedings throughout the day. She suggested that we start waking him again at night. My stomach just about flipped. *What!? Wake my baby, who is sleeping through the night and has SUCH good habits!?* It just didn't seem right. I talked to my husband about it and felt sick to my stomach. I felt sick that our baby wasn't gaining weight and hated the idea of waking him when we'd all worked so hard and he'd done so well with sleeping.

My husband suggested supplementing with bottles again. It was perfect. His sleep didn't have to be interrupted. And I had the perfect addition to that plan. In order to gain some insight on what was really going on, I ordered a digital baby scale online. It arrived two days later, and I started doing weighted feeds. I weighed our son, breastfed him, and weighed him again. After subtracting the weights, I knew what he'd had to drink in ounces. I did this for two days and didn't change a thing—no bottles were offered yet. I wanted to get the real picture of what had been happening.

Our son was eating about 15 ounces of milk per day. He was supposed to be getting closer to 24 ounces in a 24-hour period. My heart just about sank. Our son was hungry and not telling us. Our doctor informed us that babies can just get used to being offered less food and be content.

We started supplementing, and he took the bottles effortlessly. The same bottles he'd refused to drink months before, he was gulping down now. Gosh, I felt like a horrible mother in that moment. My baby wasn't getting enough food. His growth had fallen off of the charts. My milk supply was horrible, and I'd had no idea.

That's the thing with breastfeeding. You just don't know. You rely on your baby's cues to tell you if they are hungry. He wasn't asking for food, *ever*. He wasn't waking up early out of hunger. He seemed content and full and well fed.

Why Do I Tell You This Story?

Three reasons.

First, there are going to be people out there that tell me the schedule was to blame for our son's lack of weight gain. I want to address this upfront. To begin with, the NICU put him on a schedule. All preemies are put on a schedule. It ensures that they get enough food. Schedules are so vital to making sure preemies get what they need.

Our daughter was put on a 2-hour schedule when she was born at 37 weeks, and our son was put on a 3-hour schedule after being born at 34 weeks. That's what doctors recommend when babies are born early, and it is 100% what NICUs do. When home, our son was not taking extra supplementation when offered after breastfeeding. He didn't want any more food. Somewhere along the line, my supply tanked. He still wasn't asking for more food. I certainly would have given it to him had he given any indication that he needed it.

As you'll read when you are further into this book, I make feeding schedules based on my baby's hunger and sleep cues. I do not impose a schedule and just never look back. I always recommend feeding a hungry baby. The schedules are a starting point. And then, if a baby is asking for food sooner than scheduled, it is important to make adjustments. We had worked on full feedings and been successful. He was eating for 20 minutes. We had great schedules that worked for our son. He helped to build his schedules by telling me what he needed. This *still* happened to us. It would have happened with or without schedules.

Second, I can't stress enough how important it is to make sure that you are going in for your monthly scheduled checkups with your baby's pediatrician. I am so glad we always followed the recommended schedule perfectly. We wouldn't have known otherwise. We would have gone on thinking that our baby was getting enough nourishment when, in fact, he wasn't.

Third, I want to tell you what I did to fix the issue. I saw the data written down next to the scale I'd purchased. I kept looking at it, and I realized something. I was always going to be nervous if I continued breastfeeding. This meant I was always going to have to rely on the scale for data or I was going to have to pump before feeding him. I also knew that my body didn't respond to pumping very well. And I knew that I'd be stressed being a slave to the scale. Stress can negatively impact milk supply.

I returned the scale that we'd used for two days. I put my breast pump away. I stocked up on bottles and bought formula. We didn't look back. Our son climbed back up on the growth chart immediately with a healthy percentile. He took 24 ounces of formula during the day from bottles almost perfectly. We were all stress free knowing that he was well fed.

He continued sleeping through the night and continued with his amazing naps.

It was emotional to give up breastfeeding. I felt like I'd failed. It was the best thing for all of us, though. Do what you need to do for your family—breast, formula, pumping, a combination, whatever feels right to you. Fed is always best.

Chapter 3

2 Types of Routines to Set Up Immediately

There are two types of routines that you should start incorporating from day one of your baby's entrance into the world. Both routines encourage and help to prioritize sleep for your baby.

Nap and Night Routines

Do you have a routine before going to bed?

If so, it probably helps you sleep. Maybe you change into your pajamas, then brush your teeth, and then read a chapter in your latest novel.

You've learned over the years how to settle yourself in for the night and prepare your body for sleep.

Babies benefit from this type of simple routine as well.

Choose a routine that you do with your baby before *every nap* and *every night's sleep*. (Nap routines may not have time to happen until your baby is closer to 3–4 weeks old.)

These sleep routines help to tell your baby that it is time to sleep. The consistency of doing the routine before every nap and at bedtime helps to mentally prepare your baby for sleep.

The neat thing you'll start to notice is that your baby will know, just by the start of the routine, that it's time for sleep!

The simple act of walking upstairs and into their bedroom told both of our babies that it was nap time. In the early months, they'd snuggle into me. Later, they had moments of protesting immediately. Either way, I could tell they *knew* it was nap time. And that is a huge win!

From there, we kept it SUPER simple. If you keep the routine short and simple, you can do it anytime, anywhere. And you can get your baby to sleep *quickly*.

I like to keep the routine very rigid in the first couple of months when babies are just learning things. Everything happens in the same order. I even read the same book every single night. I think my husband thought I was a bit crazy! I literally, for 8 months straight, read the same book to my child. The consistency helps tremendously.

Just remember three words: **Simple. Consistent. Quick.**

And then, make a routine that works for you...

Sample Nap Routine

Change diaper.

I like to start every nap time with a fresh diaper. This just helps to make sure your baby is comfortable and doesn't wake early unnecessarily.

Place your baby in swaddle.

For newborns to 3-months of age, always swaddle. This helps your baby feel secure. Babies have what's called a moro reflex. It's what causes them to suddenly jump awake and flail their arms out. They move their arms and suddenly feel like they are falling. It startles them enough that they wake. Swaddling them helps to keep their arms in and prevents them from startling awake.

My favorite swaddle is called the SwaddleUp. Both of our babies loved it. It keeps a baby's arms above his/her head in a very comfortable and natural position. The best part is that the arms of the swaddle zip off. This means that, when you are ready to unswaddle, you can do so one arm at a time and ease your baby into the transition.

For newborns (1–2 months of age), I always suggest the full swaddle (both arms in). Every nap. Every night. Starting in months 2 and 3, phase out the swaddle (one arm at a time), and eventually replace it with a sleep sack. By 4 months old, our babies were completely transitioned out of the swaddle.

Close curtains and turn out lights.

Room darkening curtains help a ton to provide your baby with a good sleeping environment. Have the curtains open for wake time, and then close them as a part of the nap and bedtime routine. Then turn the lights off. These two things are just extra steps that your baby notices and starts to correlate with sleep.

Turn on sound machine.

Babies are used to a lot of noise when in the womb. It's really hard to go from that noisy environment to a perfectly quiet one and be expected to sleep. Use a sound machine to help comfort your baby.

Side note: I highly recommend using a sound machine. A sound machine won't become a sleep crutch (meaning your child must have it in order to sleep).

It WILL, however, become a sleep association. So, when on vacation in a new place, you can take the sound machine along and use it to indicate to your child it's time to sleep. It is a phenomenal tool to use!

I go into more detail about the use of sleep tools, like sound machines, in the appendix section.

Tell your baby it's nap time.

One of the most important things to remember is that your baby is learning. Don't forget to tell your baby that it's nap time and time to sleep. Your child may not know what that means, but he/she will learn over time. So, go ahead and tell your baby what's going on.

Give hugs.

Take a moment. Give your baby some kisses and hugs. Snuggle and hold your child. Don't get comfortable, and don't take too long. But give your baby some love. Take a deep breath and feel your body relax. Your baby will learn to do the same. If you are feeling relaxed, your baby will feel relaxed. Take a couple of minutes to do this.

Do not rock your baby. Do not bounce. Do not put your baby to sleep. You want your baby awake, but relaxed, and even drowsy is ok. Eyes open though!

We made the mistake of rocking our oldest daughter to sleep. It is a hard habit to break. Things went much more smoothly with our son since we decided up front to not do this. It was perfect, and we were so glad we made that decision. He learned to put himself to sleep easily since we weren't getting in his way.

I think that's such an important thing to realize—babies can learn to put themselves to sleep. We get in the way of them doing that at times. If we have them set up successfully, they can and will do it pretty easily!

So, remember: hugs to relax and get him/her in a calm state, but keep your baby awake.

Place in safe sleep environment.

After this quick routine, you simply place your baby into the crib or bassinet. Walk out of the room and let your child sleep!

Sample Bedtime Routine

There are only a couple of differences when it comes to the bedtime routine. First, the bedtime routine includes a bottle. This bottle will be one that you keep until your baby turns 1. It is typically the last bottle to go as it helps relax your baby for the night. Second, you can take the time to incorporate something extra, maybe a book or a bath. I still recommend keeping the same rule, however: **Simple. Consistent. Quick.** You still want this to be a routine that you can do anywhere, anytime.

I highly recommend not having bath as a part of the routine. I make this recommendation for a few reasons. One, your baby doesn't need a bath every day. Frequent bathing dries out the skin. We bathe our babies maybe 1–2 times a week unless they need it before that for some reason. Second, it makes the routine long. Third, it isn't something that you can reliably do anywhere. If you do incorporate a bath, do it first thing so it's not something your baby heavily relies on to relax and you can drop it if need be.

Change diaper.

Start the night with a fresh diaper. The hope is that it lasts all night and you won't be changing it again until morning. For newborns, I do this step first so the act of changing their diaper doesn't wake them up too much after a nice relaxing bottle and a book. In the later months, it won't matter when you do this step, however.

Feed (bottle/nurse).

For bedtime, the last feed of the day is part of the sleep routine. Make sure you keep your baby awake and get a full feed using the tactics discussed in Chapter 2. Also, make sure you get a burp out of your baby. Gas is a common culprit in keeping babies awake. I've found with both of my children that pressing and rubbing in an upwards or circular motion on their backs is way better than the typical pat method.

Read book(s).

Starting around month 2, start incorporating a book into the routine. Your baby may not even be looking at the book, but the act of reading is still valuable. Babies relax when they hear the rhythm of your voice, and they start getting used to the very healthy habit of reading. I read the same book every night to provide consistency.

Starting around month 4, read two books instead of just one. Vary the first book and always end with the book you've been reading since birth. Somewhere around month 9 or 10 it is not nearly as important to be this rigid with book choice, but your baby may still prefer the consistency.

Place your baby in swaddle.

As discussed earlier, swaddle your baby until month 4, wean them off of the swaddle, and then use a sleep sack. Make sure the temperature is good for a full night's sleep.

Close curtains and turn out lights.

Obviously, you want it nice and dark at bedtime. The room darkening curtains help when your baby is going to bed at a healthy, early bedtime. (See the schedules chapter for recommended times.)

Turn on sound machine.

Use the sound machine all night. Even keep it on when doing a night feed.

Tell your baby it's bedtime.

Again, tell your baby it's bedtime. This time, I also recommend telling your baby that you will see him/her in the morning. This helps to differentiate it from nap time and sets the expectation that you will be in when it's time to get up for the day.

Give hugs.

Take a couple of minutes to help your baby relax. Give hugs and kisses, and keep your baby awake.

Place in a safe sleep environment.

Always place your baby on his/her back in a bassinet or crib with no blankets, pillows or loveys for the safest sleep environment.

Sample Nap Routine
Change diaper.
Place your baby in swaddle.
Close curtains and turn out lights.
Turn on sound machine.
Tell your baby it's nap time.
Give hugs.
Place in safe sleep environment.

Sample Bedtime Routine
Change diaper.
Feed (bottle/nurse).

Read book(s).
Place your baby in swaddle.
Close curtains and turn out lights.
Turn on sound machine.
Tell your baby it's bedtime.
Give hugs.
Place in safe sleep environment.

Once your baby is around 4 months old, start to vary the order of both the nap and night routines. I find that this teaches babies how to be flexible while still providing the consistency they need. When you do this, anyone can do the routine. A babysitter can do the routine if need be. The order might vary and the style might be different, but if the steps all take place, your baby will still know it is bedtime.

Eat, Wake, Sleep Routines

The second important routine to teach your child is the eat, wake, sleep routine. This is a routine that is incorporated throughout the day, all day.

How It Works

Feed your baby, then have some awake time, then let your child sleep. Then wake your baby up and repeat eat, wake, sleep throughout the day, always in that order.

Why Is This Important?

Babies that eat and then fall asleep immediately learn to associate sleep with eating. They become reliant on eating in order to fall asleep. Eating can quickly become a crutch needed to fall asleep. It is soothing and relaxing to babies.

Babies won't get full feeds if they are falling asleep while eating, however, and they will be relying on food to help them get to sleep. This is NOT what you want. You want your baby to learn to fall asleep without being fed. Otherwise, every time your child wakes up at night, you'll be running in to feed your child.

Your baby won't be hungry at these middle-of-the-night feedings. Rather, your baby will be essentially using you, or the bottle, as a pacifier. If you want to encourage good sleep habits, separating feedings from sleep will be one of your first huge successes!

Now, babies still need food at night for the first couple of months, so follow your baby's lead and feed when necessary. You can challenge your child, however, as I'll discuss in Chapter 6.

By 4 months of age, however, if your baby is getting enough food during the day, he/she will no longer need night feedings. When (if) your baby does wake up at night, it is safe to assume it's more out of habit than anything, or perhaps your child is still learning to transition sleep cycles.

The good news is that if you have an eat, wake, sleep cycle set up during the day, your baby will be well on his/her way to being able to put *him/herself* to sleep without needing food!

Chapter 4

*The Eat, Wake, Sleep Cycle
Explained*

The eat, wake, sleep cycle is an invaluable tool for parents of newborns through 1 year of age. It will help your baby sleep better and will make your days go smoothly and predictably. Whether you have an 11-month-old or a little one that's just a few months old, *or even a few weeks old*, your child will benefit from this easy routine.

The Eat, Wake, Sleep Cycle

Let's talk about this routine a bit more in depth. A routine is defined as a sequence of actions that is regularly followed. This routine is more than just a sleep schedule. In fact, you can technically do the "routine" without being on any sort of schedule, *although I wouldn't recommend that.*

What Is the Eat, Wake, Sleep Cycle?

Eat, wake, sleep cycles indicate a particular order to follow throughout the day. Basically, your baby eats, then has awake time, and then has time to sleep. You then repeat the cycle throughout the day.

This cycle is often abbreviated EWS and might also be referred to as an eat, *play*, sleep cycle or a *feed*, wake, sleep cycle. It's all the same.

The Purpose of the EWS Cycle

The main purpose of this cycle is to prevent your child from doing a play, **eat, sleep** routine. If your child is accustomed to eating before sleeping, it can create a bit of a sleep crutch or sleep prop (meaning he/she relies on eating in order to fall asleep). The act of inserting wake time in between eating and sleeping helps to combat that sleep crutch.

It also tremendously aids in having a smooth bedtime routine and can help in avoiding difficult sleep training methods. We'll talk more about this below when discussing the benefits of the eat, wake, sleep cycle, however.

The Parts of the EWS Routine

Eat

This is obviously when feeding occurs. This should occur right when your baby wakes up from a nap (within a few minutes is fine).

Wake

This is any awake time and happens after eating. However, when figuring out schedules and total times, it technically includes the time babies spend eating as well as playing, engaging, etc. But, don't worry, we'll discuss that further in the schedules chapter.

Sleep

Time spent sleeping each cycle. This occurs *after* wake time.

What Are the Benefits of the EWS Cycle?

Establish Day and Night

With this routine, you are keeping your baby active during the day and waking him/her when it is time to eat.

At the newborn phase, you are *actively* keeping your baby awake pretty much at all times during the eat and wake portions of the cycle. At night, let your child sleep as long as possible (unless directed otherwise by your baby's pediatrician). The absence of the routine is a cue to sleep longer stretches.

Full Feedings

Newborns are notorious for taking short feeds and snacking. They then fall asleep and wake up starving. The EWS method promotes full feedings by helping to prevent the newborn short feeds.

With this routine, babies only have certain times to eat each cycle. They will get used to taking full feedings instead of snacking whenever they want. They learn that feeding time is time to eat.

Sleep Success

Babies learn from this routine when it is time to sleep. They learn to fall asleep without being fed to sleep. They sleep throughout the day and get healthy naps which, in turn, sets them up for success at night.

Putting the work in to combine the eat, wake, sleep routine with a schedule will tremendously help your baby.

If babies are kept awake too long, becoming overtired, they will wake early from naps (usually around 30 minute naps). If babies are kept awake for too little time and are undertired, they will wake early from naps as well. Finding the right schedule will help your baby take nice long, effective naps.

If the schedules are too much, however, the eat, wake, sleep routine can help a great deal on its own with setting your baby up for sleep success.

We all hear the comments that you should never wake a sleeping baby. I know it feels weird when you do it, but I am so thankful that I put those comments out of sight and out of mind. The combination of the eat, wake, sleep routine and schedules made us truly successful with our babies.

We'll discuss finding the right schedule for your baby in the next chapter.

Predictability

Even 2-week-olds benefit from having consistency in their lives. They start to learn that they eat right after waking up from a nap, then get some awake time, and then it's nap time again. Babies thrive on the predictability of the routine.

Because you know when your baby will be awake, you can plan your day much better.

Smooth Bedtime Routine

Night is so key to having a good day. And day is so key to having a good night.

If you can get your baby to sleep quickly and easily, nights will go better. Sleep begets sleep. The more sleep your child gets at night, the better your child's sleep will be during the day and vice versa. Having an eat, wake, sleep cycle, and wake time between feedings helps your baby learn to fall asleep on their own and helps bedtime happen more easily.

Sleep Training Will Be Easier

When your baby learns to fall asleep without being nursed or bottle fed, if he/she wakes in the middle of the night, your baby won't need to be fed in order to fall back asleep (unless actually hungry).

Enough said right? This is the first big step towards your baby sleeping well and being able to self-soothe and fall back asleep at night. That's a win-win!

The term "sleep training" is one that is often misunderstood. Technically, everything you are doing in this book to promote good sleep habits is sleep training. You are teaching, or training, your baby how to sleep well, how to go to sleep on his/her own, how to sleep without needing to be fed, how to transition sleep cycles, when to sleep, and even how much sleep is needed to set up good sleep habits.

So often, however, we are led to believe that sleep training simply means using cry it out techniques. The use of cry it out techniques are going to be very minimal if you use the methods outlined in this book. Odds are, you won't need to use cry it out methods at all.

Chapter 5

Get Your Baby on a Feeding & Sleeping Schedule

Ok, so, you've established day from night. You've worked with your baby on getting full feedings. You've established routines for naps and bedtime. And you've gotten the eat, wake, sleep routine down during the day. This last step ties everything all together. It gives you a focus and specific goals throughout the day. It makes sure that your baby gets just the right amount of wake time and sleep time during the day to be successful at night.

This Last Step Is to Create a Schedule.

That's right, you are going to look at the clock—all day long! The magic happens when you put all of this hard work and all of these amazing techniques together. You've given your baby the tools to be successful in the previous chapters. Now, with the use of schedules, you are directing your baby and tying it all together.

Notice I mention that you are *directing* your baby. We direct our children on the right behaviors, to say please and thank you, how to use a spoon, when to go potty, etc. We teach our children and expect to give them direction as they get older. The same needs to hold true for the baby stages.

We need to be the ones deciding when and how much our babies will sleep and how much wake time our babies need. We, as parents, know best. The idea here is that we aren't leaving it up to our babies. We are using cues from them, along with knowledge of what babies their age need, and making educated decisions on their behalf. We are *parenting*.

The schedule ensures that your baby is getting the right amount of:

- Feedings

- Wake time
- Sleep throughout the day
- Sleep throughout the night

Full feedings, day versus night, and routines won't matter one bit if you have an overtired baby. Nope. It won't matter for a second. An overtired baby is a VERY unhappy baby. An undertired baby is also unhappy if you try to put him/her to sleep! The schedule ensures that there is a balance of wake time and sleep. It is essential to success.

Every child is different. So, when you look at the sample schedules, keep that in mind. These are the basic schedules my husband and I used with our two children. These schedules are a starting point for you. You will need to tweak them, however, to work for your unique child. Your child might be a month behind or a month ahead. Maybe your baby is doing more wake time or slightly less. These schedules are a guide and a great place to start.

How to Implement a Schedule

The sample schedules provided are based on the eat, wake, sleep cycles. Feeding times indicate the time that you will wake and feed (nursing or bottle) your baby. Then you will have wake time, and then your baby will go down for a nap until the next feeding time.

For the first month, I do not list specific times for naps. Babies have very minimal wake time, and it is more stressful to try and schedule naps at that age than to just go with the flow. The newborn schedule during the first month is just a goal. It will feel like it's all over the place with wake times and naps, so don't even stress about it—just focus on feeding at the right times and doing the order of eat, wake, sleep throughout the day with each cycle. In month 2, however, you'll start to see specific nap times listed. Your baby can handle more of a schedule at this point and will be more predictable.

Let's take a look at a schedule (from the table at the end of this chapter) and walk through the idea together.

I'll use the 2-month schedule as our example here:

- <u>Feeding times:</u> 6 a.m., 9 a.m., 12 p.m., 3 p.m., 5:30 p.m., 8 p.m.
- <u>Naps:</u> 7–9 a.m., 10 a.m.–12 p.m., 1–3 p.m., 4–5:30 p.m., 6:30–7:30 p.m.
- <u>Notes:</u> Wake time is 1 hr to 1 hr 10 min. Last cycle wake is at 7:30 p.m. Have awake time, then feed at 8 p.m. and start the bedtime routine.

Starting at 6 a.m., wake your baby and nurse/give bottle. Your baby needs 1 hour of wake time at this age. Remember the feeding times count as a part of the wake time. So, 1 hour from 6 a.m., you'll be putting your baby down for the first nap. The goal for this nap is 2 hours, from 7 a.m. to 9 a.m.

If your baby needs 50 minutes of wake time instead, just adjust the schedule to start nap at 6:50 a.m. or adjust out for slightly longer wake time. 10 minutes can actually make a very big difference in the way that your baby sleeps, so you want to observe over the course of a few days and get the wake time just right. It will be somewhere around the 1 hour mark, though, at this age. You'll know if the wake time is incorrect based on how the nap goes. *If your baby wakes up early, check out the appendix section on short naps to find out how to troubleshoot and deal with this.*

At 9 a.m., if your baby is still sleeping, you will need to wake your child for a feeding. It feels weird to wake your baby up at first, but just keep in mind that you are doing it for good reasons.

1. You need to cap the sleep during the day so your baby doesn't get too much. Remember you'd much rather have long stretches of sleep at night.
2. You need to make sure you get your baby enough food throughout the day.

So, get your baby up at 9 a.m. Nurse or feed a bottle at that time. Then have your second awake time for the day. After the wake time of 1 hour has elapsed, put your baby down at 10 a.m. for the second nap of the day. Wake at 12 p.m. for a feeding. Nap again from 1 p.m. to 3 p.m., wake to feed at 3 p.m. Nap again at 4 p.m., this time wake at 5:30 p.m. to feed.

Now you get into the last cycle of the day, right before bed. Your baby takes a nap from 6:30 to 7:30 p.m. and wakes at 7:30 p.m., but don't feed quite yet. Have some play time instead. Maybe do a relaxing bath at this time, but keep it engaging. This last cycle, you are essentially doing *wake*, *eat*, sleep, instead of eat, wake, sleep—but don't worry, it's ok to do!

At 8 p.m., you are going to start your bedtime routine. The bedtime routine should start with a bottle/nursing session. Then do the rest of the routine. This ensures that your baby is not falling asleep while eating. The feeding at this time is relaxing and soothing. It helps your child prepare for sleep and, since you are doing the rest of the routine after the feeding, your baby will not be relying on the feeding as a sleep crutch.

Get your baby ready, and place him/her down for bed no later than 8:30 p.m. You also don't have to stall until 8:30 p.m. if your routine goes faster than 30 minutes. Just get your baby down when you are done.

Start the next day with the same 6 a.m. wake time, regardless of how the night goes—*even if your baby wakes up at 4:30 a.m.* Follow the steps in the next chapter to deal with nighttime waking. If you feed your baby, put him/her back down, and then wake up again at 6 a.m. The consistency of the morning wake time sets the entire day up for success.

*Pro tip: Use the alarm clock on your phone to alert you of feeding times and nap times!

Starting Schedules

Now, after reading all of these sample schedules, you might be thinking, "Ok, but where do I start!?"

Don't stress. Just start.

You can't be successful if you don't begin. Find your baby's age on the chart. Implement the schedule. Take notes.

You can download a printable version of the schedules shown at this link:

https://printableparentingtools.mamasorganizedchaos.com

I recommend printing the schedules out and laminating them. Record your observations and take note of short naps, tired signs, etc. Observe for at least 3 days, and then make changes based on what your baby seems to need.

Make one change at a time. See what that does. The schedule will go smoothly if it's the right schedule for *your baby*.

Also, take a look at this chart of the **average wake times** for babies by age. Your baby might need more or less wake time than my babies did! This chart is a great way to look at the averages for each age range. You'll notice that my sample schedules vary from this a bit because of what we experienced with our unique children.

Age	Cycle Length	# of Cycles	Wake Time per Cycle	# of Naps
1-2 weeks	2 hours	8	Minimal	N/A
3-4 weeks	2.5-3 hours	6-7	1 hour	N/A
2 months	3 hours	6-7	1-1hour 10 min	5-6
3 months	2.5-3 hours	5	1.5 hours	4
4 months	3-4 hours	5	2 hours	3
5 months	3.5-4 hours	4	2 hours	3
6 months	4.5 hours	4	2.5-3 hours	2-3
7 months	4.5 hours	3	2.5-3 hours	2
8 months	4.5-5 hours	3	3-3.5 hours	2
9 months	4.5-5 hours	3	3-3.5 hours	2
10 months	5-5.5 hours	3	3-5.5 hours	1-2
11 months	5-5.5 hours	3	3-5.5 hours	1-2
12 months	5-5.5 hours	3	3-5.5 hours	1-2

Cycle length indicates the time of one full eat, wake, sleep cycle. Wake time includes eating times. This chart is based on our personal experience and sleep charts found at (My Baby Sleep Guide, n.d.)

Weaning Off of Nursing/Bottles

The goal during the first 12 months is to slowly wean your child from bottles or nursing sessions. You'll notice that this slow progression happens easily over the course of 12 months, dropping one feeding at a time and eventually adding in solid foods. It's a natural progression as you add in more wake time, less naps, and include solid foods.

By 12 months, your baby is on one bedtime bottle/nursing session. When you and your baby are ready, that will be easy to replace with whole milk.

A Note About Bedtime

You'll notice that each schedule ends with a feeding. This is the last feeding of the day, and it is the *start* of the bedtime routine.

The routine is flipped from eat, wake, sleep to wake, eat, sleep. Just make sure you don't let your baby fall asleep while eating. The goal is to feed before bed and then do the bedtime routine (books, bath, etc.).

Example: If the last feeding is 6:30 p.m., unless otherwise noted, this is also bedtime. Do the feeding, and then go right into your bedtime routine and put your baby down. Your routine, including bottle, should take no longer than 30 minutes.

Scheduling Roadblocks

I strongly believe that the first year of a baby's life should be given priority when it comes to the family as a whole. Little babies just really need their sleep, food, and routines. If we are constantly disrupting them, it's just not fair to them and we aren't setting them up for success. For this reason, a lot of things take a back seat the first year. I didn't plan as many outings with our older daughter. I did things at home instead.

Now, there are also things that simply can't be avoided, especially if you have older children. There are school drop-off times and school pick-up times. There are ballet classes and soccer practice. There are doctor appointments and all sorts of things.

So, when I get to *choose* the timing of something (like an appointment), I try to schedule it when my baby will be awake. It's ok to alter the schedule a bit, but if I can take my baby out during wake time, it will make for a much smoother outing. I might have to wake my baby up early or put my baby down a tiny bit late, but those things are ok! Just do what you can to keep your baby's schedule on track as best you can. Also, know that one day with an interruption is not the end of the world. Babies on schedules actually become pretty flexible because they know what to expect. They know that their food is still coming, and they will get caught up on sleep—*no worries.*

When it comes to things that we have no control over, however, we simply have to figure out a new plan. School times are not something we get to decide. When our son was just a newborn, he was having to do a lot of napping on the go for school drop-off and pick-up times. It just was what it was, and I couldn't do anything about it.

The Problem We Had to Solve:

Our 4-year-old daughter started Pre-K, and our 8-month-old had to get his schedule altered as a result. Our daughter had to be dropped off at school at 1 p.m. and picked up at 3:20 p.m. 5 days a week. Our son was on a schedule that had him sleeping from 2:30 p.m. to 4:30 p.m. Clearly that wasn't going to work. I'd be putting him down at 2:30 p.m., waking him up at 3 p.m., and transferring him to the car knowing full well he would not be going to go back to sleep. As a result, I changed his schedule *completely*.

When things like this arise, I keep in mind one thing: *total daytime sleep*. I needed to somehow get him roughly the same amount of daytime sleep but rearrange the schedule to something he could handle. If you take a look at the recommended 8-month-old schedule (in the chart on the following pages), you will see that there are two naps that occur from 9:30 a.m. to 11:30 a.m. and 2:30 p.m. to 4:30 p.m. This is a total of 4 hours of daytime sleep. I figured out a new schedule that was going to work with our daughter's school timing, keeping that total daytime sleep in mind.

Solving the Problem and Altering the Recommended Schedule

Old Schedule

- Feeding times: 7 a.m., 11:30 a.m., 4:30 p.m., 6:30 p.m.
- Naps: 9:30–11:30 a.m., 2:30–4:30 p.m.
- Total daytime sleep: 4 hours

New Schedule

- Feeding times: 7 a.m., 11:00 a.m., 3:30 p.m., 6:30 p.m.
- Naps: 9 –11 a.m., 1:30–3 p.m.
- Total daytime sleep: 3.5 hours

I gave our son a feeding at 7 a.m. as usual and the first nap was moved to an *earlier* time. He'd then get his second feeding at 11 a.m. and we'd go to school drop-off at 1 p.m. When we arrived home at 1:30 p.m. he'd go down for a nap. At 3 p.m. I woke him up. I *did not* feed him because there wasn't time.

We'd go pick up his big sister, and then we'd head home. If I had fed him before pick-up, I would have needed to wake him earlier than 3 p.m. and his nap would have been cut too short. So, the EWS routine was altered a bit and I had him do a wake, eat, wake, sleep routine for that cycle.

He was given a bottle at 3:30 p.m. and would stay awake until bedtime at 6:30 p.m. This was a much longer stretch of awake time than he was used to. If it was too hard for him, he went down for bed at 6 p.m. instead of 6:30 p.m. He got used to the new stretch of time quickly, however. Total daytime sleep with the altered schedule was still 3.5 hours, only 30 minutes less than the ideal schedule.

I mention all of this because I want you to know that having to have a schedule that is not "perfect" is ok. Your baby will adjust. There are just some things we can't work around. So, we have to make a new plan. That's ok. Just figure out the new plan, prioritize that daytime sleep as best you can, and give it a try.

Sample Schedules

(Feeding times refer to bottle/nursing sessions)

Newborn 1–2 Weeks
- Minimal wake time
- Feeding times: 6 a.m., 9 a.m., 12 p.m., 3 p.m., 6 p.m., 9 p.m.
- Nap times will vary greatly, so do not worry about a schedule for naps at this point.

- If you are instructed by your doctor to wake at night, wake at 12 a.m. and 3 a.m. Preemies will need to be woken up and fed.
- Focus on full feedings and the eat, wake, sleep cycle.

Newborn 3–4 Weeks

- 35–50 minutes wake time
- <u>Feeding times</u>: 6 a.m., 9 a.m., 12 p.m., 3 p.m., 6 p.m., 9 p.m.
- Nap times will vary greatly as your baby is adjusting to more wake time.
- Focus on full feedings and the eat, wake, sleep cycle.

Month 2

- Wake time 1–1 hour 10 minutes
- <u>Feeding times</u>: 6 a.m., 9 a.m., 12 p.m., 3 p.m., 5:30 p.m., 8 p.m.
- <u>Naps</u>: 7–9 a.m., 10–12 p.m., 1–3 p.m., 4–5:30 p.m., 6:30–7:30 p.m.
- Last cycle wake at 7:30 p.m., then have awake time, then feed at 8 p.m., and then start bedtime routine.

Month 3

- Wake time 1.5 hours
- <u>Feeding times</u>: 6:30 a.m., 10 a.m., 1 p.m., 4 p.m., 7 p.m.
- <u>Naps</u>: 8–10 a.m., 11:30–1 p.m., 2:30–4 p.m., 5:30–6:30 p.m.
- Last cycle wake at 6:30 p.m., then have awake time, then feed at 7 p.m., and then start bedtime routine.

Month 4

- Wake time 1.5–2 hours
- <u>Feeding times</u>: 6:30 a.m., 10 a.m., 1 p.m., 4 p.m., 7 p.m.
- <u>Naps</u>: 8–10 a.m., 11:30–1 p.m., 2:30–4 p.m., 5:30–6:30 p.m.
- Last cycle wake at 6:30 p.m., then have awake time, then feed at 7 p.m., and then start bedtime routine.

Months 5 & 6

- Wake time 2 hours
- <u>Feeding times</u>: 7 a.m., 11 a.m., 3 p.m., 7:20 p.m. (offer solids *after* bottles for breakfast, lunch, and dinner)
- <u>Naps</u>: 9–11 a.m., 1–3 p.m., 5–5:50 p.m.
- Last cycle wake at 5:50 p.m., and do not offer a bottle. Offer solids for dinner and have wake time. At 7:20 p.m., do bedtime bottle and bedtime routine.

Month 7

- Wake time 2 hours 15 minutes
- <u>Feeding times</u>: 7 a.m., 11 a.m., 3:30 p.m., 7:20 p.m. (offer solids *after* bottles for breakfast, lunch, and dinner)
- <u>Naps</u>: 9:15–11 a.m., 1:15–3 p.m., 5:30–6 p.m.
- Last cycle wake at 6 p.m., and do not offer a bottle. Offer solids and have wake time. At 7:20 p.m., do bedtime bottle and bedtime routine.

Month 8

- Wake time 2–3 hours

- Wake times vary throughout the day now as you move to a 2-nap schedule.
- <u>Feeding times</u>: 7 a.m., 11:30 a.m., 4:30 p.m., 6:30 p.m. (offer solids *after* bottles for breakfast, lunch, and dinner)
- <u>Naps</u>: 9:30–11:30 a.m., 2:30–4:30 p.m.

Month 9

- Wake time 3–3.5 hours
- As you push wake time to be longer, naps push out a bit and so does bedtime. You can also make the transition to solids *before* bottles for some meals. I usually start with lunch this month and then slowly add the others one month at a time.
- <u>Feeding times</u>: 7 a.m., 12 p.m., 4:30 p.m., 6: 30 p.m. (offer solids *before* bottles for breakfast, lunch, and dinner)
- <u>Naps</u>: 10–12 p.m., 3:30–4:30 p.m.

Month 10

- Wake time 3–3.5 hours
- <u>Feeding times</u>: 7 a.m., 4:30 p.m., 6:30 p.m. (offer solids *before* bottles for breakfast, lunch, and dinner)
- <u>Naps</u>: 10–12 p.m., 3:30–4:30 p.m.
- Notice you drop the lunch bottle here and are down to 3 bottles/nursing sessions now.

Month 11

- Wake time 3–3.5 hours *or* 5.5 hours
- Your baby may transition to 1 nap this month.
- Down to 2 bottle/nursing sessions.

- Feeding times: 7 a.m., 6:30 p.m. (offer solids for breakfast, lunch, and dinner)
- 2 nap schedule: 10–12 p.m., 3–4 p.m.
- 1 nap schedule: 12:30–3 p.m.

Month 12

- Wake time 3–3.5 hours *or* 5.5 hours
- Your baby may transition to 1 nap this month.
- Down to 1 bottle/nursing session.
- Feeding times: 6:30 p.m. (offer solids for breakfast, lunch, and dinner)
- 2 nap schedule: 10–12 p.m., 3–4 p.m.
- 1 nap schedule: 12:30–3 p.m.

Chapter 6

How to Tackle Nighttime Wakings
in 6 Easy Steps

These are the 6 things to keep in mind when dealing with night wakings. My husband and I found such great success with these, and dropping nighttime feedings became a simple task. You can only focus on dropping nighttime feedings, however, if your baby's days are going well. So, don't attempt to implement any sort of system at night until you have your baby feeding well and have your routines and schedules in place. And, remember, babies do need some food throughout the night in the early stages.

With that said, even during those early weeks, when your baby needs food at night, you can focus on dealing with the feedings in a way that shows your baby it's still a time to sleep and go back to bed.

Always Feed Your Newborn Baby

Don't even think twice about it. Babies need food. Expect it and be ok with it so you don't get yourself stressed. Expecting a baby to just automatically sleep at night is like expecting a toddler not to have accidents while potty training. Night wakings are a part of being a baby. They happen. They do not have to go on longer than 4 months, though. Wrap your mind around that goal, and then keep reading on how to best handle it.

Get Your Baby on a Feeding Schedule During the Day

Refer to the sample schedules and start working to find the ideal schedule for your baby. You can start focusing on good sleep habits at any age, so don't stress if you are starting with an older baby.

Keep your daily schedule in mind at nighttime. If your baby can go 3 hours during the day between feedings, your baby can go 3 hours at night. Challenge your child to do so by stalling the feeding with a pacifier or putting him/her back to sleep however you can. If this doesn't work, however…feed your baby. Don't let your baby wake up too much.

Do Not Change Your Baby's Diaper Unless You Need To

Changing a diaper usually wakes and stimulates your baby. It is best to avoid this if possible. You will want to change the diaper before feeding, *if you are going to change it*. That way your baby is nice and relaxed after the feeding and ready to sleep. But, if you can get away with it, don't even bother to change it—this way your baby will stay sleepy for the feeding and go back to sleep easily.

Keep Your Baby Sleepy

Get in and out. You will stay sleepy and so will your baby. Everyone will go back to sleep more easily. That's a huge win and helps to establish day from night. As a first time mom, I thought I had to stall the feeding first and foremost. I ended up waking up our child as a result, and it was so difficult to get her back to sleep (and myself). Now I know better. Just feed your baby and everyone goes right back to sleep. I'll discuss some stalling techniques below that are successful when used correctly.

For this step, focus on keeping your baby sleepy. Your child should be awake just enough to eat. That means no unswaddling, no changing diapers, no talking, and no lights. Keep it dark, keep it quiet. Feed and get out of there!

Challenge Your Baby to Go Longer Stretches

You want to start challenging your baby to go longer stretches at night, if possible. This is where I've come to love the use of a pacifier. Even using it with this method, your baby will not rely on it as a sleep crutch and can easily drop the pacifier by month 4.

Challenge your baby to go longer stretches by giving a pacifier and stalling the feeding as long as you can (without your baby waking too much). Once your baby shows the ability to go longer stretches, don't accept less!

If your child wakes earlier than history has shown possible, go in and give a pacifier. You are basically stalling the feeding. You are pushing it out as much as you can. Give the pacifier once. Pat your baby if they need the help. If your child wakes a second time, go ahead and feed to keep sleepy.

Do this until your baby drops feeds. Then challenge him/her on the next one, and so on.

Cap Feedings

Keep lessening the amount until your baby no longer needs the feeding. If your baby is being breastfed, offer the breast for less and less time. If your baby is on bottles, offer fewer and fewer ounces. The feedings basically become "snack" feedings. They are far from full feedings, and you'll know that your baby doesn't actually *need* the food any longer since they are getting so little. Your baby will drop the feedings very naturally while also realizing he/she doesn't need the food. Your child will just stop waking up.

Note: Once you've done the above steps consistently, if your baby doesn't naturally drop the very last feeding, I've found that ONE night of cry it out drops it immediately. I do this only when I've decreased the feeding in ounces or time as much as I can but the baby keeps waking at that one time just out of habit.

Both of my babies cried for maybe 20 minutes for one night and then slept through the night from then on. At that point, I felt comfortable letting them cry since I knew for a fact they didn't need to be fed.

Appendix

Sleep Tools & Sleep Associations

I wanted to take a moment to discuss sleep tools and sleep associations. I encourage the use of both! What you don't want is to create a sleep *crutch*. Let's talk about the difference and how I recommend putting this into practice.

Sleep Crutch

Something a baby relies on to sleep and can't sleep without. A classic example is being fed to sleep. It creates a really hard habit to break when babies NEED to be fed (simply for the comfort, not the food) in order to fall back asleep.

A pacifier can fall into this category if you aren't careful with it. Your baby can rely on the pacifier to sleep, leaving you to get up in the middle of the night to find the dropped pacifier and reinsert it, over and over and over.

Sleep Associations

Something a baby associates with sleep. It is an item that indicates to your baby that it is time to sleep. Sleep associations are great! It's like a flag waving to your baby, saying, "Now's the time! Go ahead and go to sleep."

The bedtime routine that you set up is a sleep association in its entirety. Pieces of this routine can also be strong indicators to your baby.

I highly recommend the use of a sound machine, swaddles, and sleep sacks. These items are easy to travel with, so they can ALWAYS be there for your baby as an association and a comfort.

Swaddle until about 3–4 months, and then move on to sleep sacks. Use these items consistently for every nap and bedtime.

This will create a sleep association for your baby to find comfort in and use to go to sleep more readily.

My husband and I also use a sound machine for our children during every nap and bedtime in this house. There is no rush to wean a baby off of it for any reason. I love the comfort it provides and positive sleep association that it builds. Our 4 year old still enjoys hers, and many adults find it helpful as a positive sleep tool as well.

Sleep Tools

An item that helps your baby fall asleep. My classic example is a pacifier. You can use it in a healthy way as a sleep tool by not overusing it, but also using it enough to let it actually help your baby. Just be careful not to turn it into a sleep crutch—find a good balance between being helpful and being relied upon.

How We Use a Pacifier

Always allow your baby to try and sleep without the pacifier at the start of all naps and at bedtime.

If your baby is struggling to sleep and gets upset, offer the pacifier. Only reinsert the pacifier once or twice. Decide a clear number for yourself ahead of time and stick to the plan.

If your baby wakes up early from a nap, use the pacifier to get him/her back to sleep quickly (without having to be fed). If your baby wakes up at night, stall him/her with the use of a pacifier. This can help to extend night feedings.

When used in this way, the pacifier is a helpful tool and will not become a sleep crutch.

Our first baby never took to the pacifier, but our second did. He dropped the pacifier by 4 months old and no longer used it. I felt nervous, as we used it a lot but only in the ways listed above. Because we'd allowed him to fall asleep on his own as well, and always expected him to try before giving him the pacifier, he never relied on the pacifier, and it never became something he *needed* to sleep.

The above guidelines created the perfect balance with the pacifier, and we were able to use it as a valuable tool to help him learn how to sleep.

Sleep Tools I Recommend

SwaddleUp

The SwaddleUp is a wonderful swaddle that keeps your baby's arms up above his/her head, which is often what babies prefer. It prevents your baby from startling awake, however.

Sound Machine

Any sound machine will work. Use a sound machine from day 1 at home with your new baby. Use it for every nap and all night.

Pacifier

The pacifier we prefer is the one that comes home with you from the hospital. It is the Philips Avent pacifier. Use the newborn ones and you'll never need to size up since you'll drop it by the time your baby is 4 months old.

My Tot Clock

This is a sleep tool that I start using around 18 months of age, but it is a priceless tool (and perhaps my favorite parenting item) so I wanted to mention it here. Once your child knows his/her colors, this tool becomes invaluable for aiding in explaining bedtime rules. The clock can be set to turn blue when bedtime starts, and yellow when it is time for your child to get up.

If you start using it at 18 months, your child will be very familiar with it by the time he/she transitions out of the crib. This one tool will keep your child in bed and make the transition seamless. The brand I like is called the My Tot Clock.

How to Handle Short Naps

One of the biggest questions from parents is how to handle short naps. Short naps can be an indication that something is bothering your baby or that the schedule needs to be changed.

Typically, a nap that is around 20–30 minutes in length indicates that your baby is <u>overtired</u>. This could be that your baby is overstimulated or that the wake time is too long.

Waking around the 45 minute mark can be caused by a wide variety of factors, including teething pain, being cold, a dirty diaper, or being undertired (and needing more wake time or more stimulation).. Babies transition sleep cycles around 45 minutes into a nap (Ezzo, 2012 5th Edition), so they enter a lighter sleep momentarily and will notice little things like dirty diapers, being cold, teething pain, etc.

Wait a few days to see if naps are consistently short before making any big changes.

How to Handle Short Naps <u>in the Moment</u>

The Happy Baby...

If your baby wakes up and is happy, always leave him/her for the full nap time, no matter what age. Quiet time is still restful time. Count it as "sleep" time and continue with your schedule.

Rules to Follow If Your Baby Is Upset

Newborn–3 Months

Allow your baby to fuss a bit. Your baby doesn't know how to self-soothe yet, so I don't recommend letting him/her cry very hard, but fussing is ok! Babies have to learn to work through this and fall asleep. Your baby might simply be transitioning sleep cycles and may not even be fully awake.

Allow Your Baby to Fuss for 5 Minutes

If crying or screaming (not just fussing), go in immediately so your baby doesn't wake up too much.

Try and get your baby back to sleep using a sleep tool. Give a pacifier. You can also try bouncing the mattress a bit or putting your hand on your baby. Do not pick up your baby. Try to get your baby back to sleep.

If your child wakes again, just get your baby up and adjust the schedule as needed.

4 Months +

This is one of my biggest tips, and it always amazes me how well it works.

Allow your baby to all-out scream and cry for 5 minutes before going in. I know that sounds harsh, but let me tell you this...

I have seen both of my babies wake up from naps and all-out scream—like red faced, gasping for air screams—and in 5 minutes they are sound asleep and take a nice long nap.

So, first of all, do yourself a favor and have a video monitor just for peace of mind that your baby truly is ok. And then, watch the clock. 5 minutes is not a long time, but it can seem like a long time in the moment. So, just watch the clock or set a timer. Decide before this happens that you are ok with a short 5 minutes of crying.

If, after 5 minutes, your baby isn't asleep, go assist with a pacifier, *shhhshing*, or patting. You can also pick your baby up and hold him/her upright without rocking or bouncing. Then put your baby back down once calm.

But the amazing thing is that, I bet, 8 of 10 times your baby will go back to sleep without you needing to go in. And, had you gone in, your baby would be wide awake, and the whole schedule for the day would be off, causing a hard night for your baby.

I'd rather have my baby cry for 5 minutes than to have lots of crying all day long because he/she is super tired and off schedule from not getting enough sleep.

If your baby is having short naps for more than 4–5 days, I would say something needs to change with the schedule. Reassess how much wake time is needed, and make sure your baby is getting lots of practice with any new skills he/she is learning before naps. Also, consider if your child might be in a growth spurt.

If you think your baby is in a growth spurt, feeding extra food may help. All will iron out in a few days if that is the case.

Take special note if your baby is learning new skills (the big ones)—sitting, crawling, pulling up, walking, or talking. These moments cause *big* sleep disruptions because babies want to get up and practice! Their minds are excited. If you notice naps are a struggle during a time when your baby is learning one of these big skills, get in lots of practice with the skill right before nap time. This will help satisfy your baby's desire to practice and ensure proper levels of physical and mental stimulation are achieved before nap time.

Nap Training

Baby Sleep Solutions

Sometimes babies just don't like to nap. As a result, sometimes parents intervene. It can be so hard to get a baby sleeping at the right times during the day. With our daughter, we really struggled with this for the first couple of months. We intervened by rocking her nearly to sleep (a drowsy state). After some thought, I came up with a pretty logical way to wean her off the rocking and for her to get good sleep during the day that ended up working really well.

I realized that my first goal was to make sure she was sleeping **at the right time.** I didn't really care how. I just wanted to make sure that she was getting enough daytime sleep to be successful at night and happy during her wake times. And so, I focused on getting her to sleep however I needed to **at the right time.**

This worked great for us. She slept in my arms, at times, or on me in a carrier. She slept in a swing, on my bed, and even on the couch. I made her nice little safe places wherever I was so I could supervise her. She slept, and we got her on the right track.

Then, once I had this down, I focused on getting her to sleep **where I wanted her to be sleeping.** This was in her bassinet as a newborn and in her crib towards the end of month 2. We had the routine down, and the schedule was going well. She was already sleeping at the right times, so I just made sure to then put her down in the correct location. This was a great next logical step and, again, it worked well.

After that, I focused on getting her to **sleep on her own.** I slowly weaned her from needing me to put her to sleep. With our daughter, we'd rocked her to a drowsy state, and oftentimes she woke up the minute we placed her in the crib. It was beyond frustrating. Around the end of month 2, I changed what I was doing for naps. I would place her in the crib and bounce the mattress to help her. I did this less and less, and eventually she was sleeping on her own, in her crib, without assistance, and *when* I wanted her to be sleeping!

This is a great way to prioritize your babies sleep needs during the day, one step at a time.

Nap Training Steps:

1. Get babies to sleep when they should be sleeping
2. Get babies to sleep where they should be sleeping
3. Get babies to sleep on their own

Just take it one step at a time, and you'll get to the ultimate goal of having your baby sleep at the right times, in the right place, and on their own.

Now, with our son we did things differently. I still recommend the above scenario, but before that, I want to give you a new goal: **don't create bad habits out of the gate.** We were so nervous with our first born that we rocked her to a drowsy state. With our son, however, we really focused on not doing that. We didn't rock at all. We did, however, make use of the pacifier as described in the sleep tools section of the appendix. It worked perfectly, and this is the method I'd use again.

From day one we were consistent with **where** he slept. We always put him down **awake**. We gave him a pacifier if he seemed to need it. As a result, we never had to go through the above steps. We never had to let him cry more than 5 minutes here and there. We placed him in his crib wide awake, and he'd go to sleep without a peep. I would 100% do this method again over the nap training steps above. It was easier on everyone, and he was taking great naps, much sooner than our daughter, as a result.

How to Know When Your Baby Needs a Schedule Change

There are four telltale ways to know if your baby needs a schedule change. You may notice just one of these or several at a time.

Naps Become Shorter

When your baby's naps suddenly start getting shorter and shorter, this can be an indication that he/she is ready for more wake time or even ready to drop a nap. You can always increase wake time or increase the amount of stimulation without doing a full schedule change. This is often the place to start before changing up the entire schedule.

Refusal to Go Down for a Nap

If your baby starts to refuse a nap all together, this can be a very clear indication that a schedule change or nap removal is needed.

Refusal to Drink a Bottle/Nurse

Refusal to drink a bottle or nurse can be an indication that your baby is ready to drop a feeding. This often coincides with adding in more wake time and rearranging nap times for a complete schedule change. Remember that you want to keep the eat, wake, sleep routines that you have worked so hard to set up!

Formula/Breast Milk Intake Lessening

If you notice that your baby is drinking less and less, this can also be an indication that it is time to drop a feeding and make a schedule change. The hard part with breastfeeding is that babies also become more efficient. So, are they just eating faster and being more efficient, or are they done faster and not eating as much? It can be hard to tell. It might require a schedule change to find out! You can always go back to an old schedule if something doesn't work out.

How to Make a Schedule Change

Have a Solid Plan

As you are noticing that your baby is in need of a schedule change, watch your baby's cues and try to figure out the scheduling changes that need to be made. Since you are making a schedule change, you are most likely dropping a nap. Drop the last nap of the day, and rearrange the schedule to accommodate longer wake times, one less nap, and one less feeding.

Also, remember that sometimes you can make wake times longer without doing a whole schedule change (meaning you'd simply start your nap a little bit later than normal).

Implement the Plan

Challenge your baby to try the new schedule. Help by keeping your baby distracted during longer wake times. Do the best you can to truly try the new schedule. If you are off slightly on the times, don't worry—just attempt it the best that you can.

Watch for Cues

Is your baby handling the change well? Are naps getting longer? Are they still short? Are they even shorter? Is your baby overtired? Too stimulated? Does it seem like your baby still needs more wake time?

Take note. This is the most important step. Look for the cues, interpret them, and trust your instincts.

Tweak

Make minor changes to your schedule as you see fit while you are implementing your plan. Give your plan some credit, though, and just make minor tweaks.

Be Consistent

You know what you are doing, so trust yourself and give your schedule a good 2–3 days of implementation before making any major changes. It may take a few days for your baby to get in the swing of things. Things could get worse before they get better. Give your baby the adjustment period.

Make Adjustments

If you are noticing after 2–3 days that things just aren't going as planned, make changes to your schedule accordingly. Don't forget that each cycle throughout the day doesn't have to be the same length. Some babies need wake times decreasing throughout the day. Others do well with shorter wake times in the morning. Do what works for your baby. Make the adjustments that you see fit.

Repeat

Repeat the above process until you feel that you have achieved a good schedule.

Take a Break If You Need To

If at any time you feel that your baby has gotten overtired and needs a break from the process, simply revert back to your old schedule and see if it can work for a day or so. This could give your baby the rest needed to make the schedule change a bit easier. It may also *not* work to do this. After all, you are making a schedule change for a reason—that old schedule wasn't quite working anymore. So, don't worry if this doesn't work out.

If it does work out, don't be afraid to have a schedule A and a schedule B. While working towards a schedule change, I've had a few periods where I needed to do schedule A for one day and schedule B for two days as a transition for our babies. This was especially true when we were transitioning from two naps to one nap.

Baby Sleep Solutions

8 Benefits of Keeping Your Baby on a Schedule

Here are the main benefits that I have seen to keeping your little one on a schedule (even if breastfeeding…in fact, *especially* if breastfeeding).

It Lessens the Detective Work When Your Baby Is Crying

When your baby cries, you will know it's not out of hunger. And, because your baby is on a nap schedule, it will be very obvious if your baby didn't get enough sleep and woke early from a nap. You will know if your baby is overtired one day. The schedules take the guesswork out of everything. It's fabulous.

Your Baby Will Be Well Fed

There are easy guidelines to follow with different age ranges and lots of resources out there. I knew that, as a newborn, our baby was going to need to be fed a minimum of 8 times throughout the day and night. The schedule allows you to fit the feedings in at appropriate times.

Your baby will also get used to the schedule and get full feedings in, as opposed to snacking all day long.

It Helps to Keep Supply Up (for Breastfeeding Mamas)

If you are nursing (or pumping) at scheduled intervals, schedules actually help to regulate your supply. If you wait until your baby asks for it, two things could happen:

First, you could get engorged throughout the day if your baby goes long intervals without asking for food, which could then cause a fast letdown. This, in turn, could make nursing difficult for your baby, especially in the early months when you are first establishing good nursing habits.

Second, you could overstimulate your supply if your baby goes short intervals and is "snack" nursing all day. This could also cause your baby to not get full feeds and to only be consuming foremilk instead of taking nice, long feedings and getting the good fuller fat hindmilk that comes towards the end of a feeding.

You (or the Bottle) Will Not Be Used as a Pacifier

Babies cry. Often when they cry, parents assume that they are crying out of hunger. With a schedule, it takes the guesswork out, and you won't end up feeding your baby at every cry. You won't end up feeling like a pacifier (if nursing), and your baby won't get used to just eating for comfort. Your baby will eat when truly hungry.

Babies Love Routine

Babies actually thrive on routine. They learn routines very well and know what to expect. Isn't your day so much easier to tackle when you know what to expect? Babies feel the same way! It is human nature to like the comfort of predictability. If you find the right schedule, your baby will be well fed, well rested, and happy during wake time.

Parents Love Routine

I was dreading getting caught out in public breastfeeding. It's fine for those that don't mind it, but I wanted privacy and to be comfortable when I was breastfeeding. I have literally only had to breastfeed in public 4 times, and it was just because I had long outings during an expected feeding time. (With our first child, we went out pretty much every day for activities, and I could easily plan around her feeding and nap times.)

I've always known when I can leave the house and that my babies will not be asking for food while we are out (or be upset because they are tired). It has made for a lot less stress for me, knowing what to expect and being able to plan around nap and feeding times.

Babies Sleep Through the Night Sooner

Babies that get enough food and the correct amount of sleep throughout the day sleep better at night. If your baby is overtired, nighttime sleep is going to be a challenge. If your baby is hungry, that can cause him/her to wake in the middle of the night for food.

It is that simple.

If you can create a schedule that allows your baby to get enough food and sleep during the day, nighttime will fall into place sooner and more easily.

Our daughter was sleeping through the night when she was 4 months old, and she was only waking out of habit during the 3rd month (not out of hunger). Our son was also sleeping through the night by 4 months old (and he was a preemie, born at 34 weeks)!

You Are Creating an Environment in Which Babies Can Learn

If your baby is well fed and well rested, your baby will be awake and happy during playtime. This allows your baby to be in a state in which he/she is ready to learn. We know it is much easier to absorb information when we are not tired and hungry. The same applies to your baby.

You'll notice that I keep mentioning "a schedule that is right for your baby." There are a lot of rumors out there about how schedules are bad for babies. I've even heard rumors so drastic that they imply you are starving your baby if you put them on a schedule. Those rumors stem from schedules being *misunderstood*.

It is not a good idea to simply impose a schedule on your baby and not listen to cues. Babies go through growth spurts, and they are simply all different in what they need. I always tell people that our children build their own schedules. I provide a starting point. I literally started by making a schedule (based on research) and trying it. But I then watched our children and all their cues. I adjusted the schedule accordingly.

Was our baby telling me she was hungry before her next scheduled feeding time? Was she tired before her nap time? Or, was she not tired enough when it came to nap time? It is very important to watch your baby and adjust the schedule to fit accordingly.

Babies will typically tell you what they need. I would observe over the course of a few days, adjusting and tweaking the schedules until I felt they were a good fit.

Once we found the right fit, we kept the schedule until I noticed it wasn't working any longer. We would then take the time to reevaluate and adjust the schedule again. Sometimes that meant dropping a feeding, dropping a nap, extending a wake time, extending a nap time, etc. You will find that a schedule typically lasts about a month before it needs a small tweak here and there.

Use the schedules section of this book to find a starting point for your baby. The schedules are great starting points, but remember, you may need to tweak the times a bit to make it a perfect fit for your little one!

Useful Resources

I found baby schedules when I was pregnant with our first born. I was scrolling through Pinterest, trying to figure out how often I was going to need to feed her. Several baby schedules popped up, and I made sure to pin them all!

I had always heard that you had to feed on demand. Schedules just fit more naturally with us, however. I wasn't sure what we were going to do when it came time since the information was so conflicting and the methods were so different. Then our daughter's pediatrician put her on a 2-hour schedule in the hospital since she was born early at 37 weeks. We loved the use of schedules and kept with it.

From there, I found the term Babywise. From there, I bought the book *On Becoming Babywise* by Gary Ezzo and Robert Bucknam. The book really fueled my passion for schedules. It's a great read. I'd highly recommend purchasing it.

After using schedules with our babies, we found specific ways to implement these tactics and ways that seemed to really build a foundation for our babies when it came to eating and sleeping habits. That's what this book is about. I wanted this book to be the real deal, the real nitty gritty with how we actually handled these things with real live babies! It sounds silly, but when you read a parenting book, it all sounds great on paper, and then doing it with your child can be a whole different ball game. Many parenting books seem to be more "philosophy," than the actual how to.

This is the how to. This is what we did. I became so passionate about prioritizing our babies sleep that I started writing about it.

More from Me

You can find all of my writings at www.mamasorganizedchaos.com. There are tons of schedule, routine, and sleep resources, along with discipline tactics, and even our potty training method!

You can find printable parenting tools that I've created here:
     printableparentingtools.mamasorganizedchaos.com

Don't forget to print out a baby schedule tracking sheet while you are there!

Parenting Books I Recommend

On Becoming Babywise and the entire "wise" series by Gary Ezzo and Rober Bucknam

The Wonder Weeks by Hetty van de Rijt and Frans Plooij

Parenting with Love and Logic by Cline and Fay

About Me

My name is Katrina Villegas. I am a former chemist, engineer, and high school teacher. I never envisioned being a stay at home mom, but as soon as that first positive pregnancy test came along, my husband and I both knew we wanted to take that path for our family.

So, here we are. I am a stay at home mom. I am applying all of my engineering, teaching, and life experiences to making my job as a stay at home mom go as smoothly as possible. My career as a stay at home mom is challenging and so rewarding. It's the best thing I've ever done.

My husband and I have 3 children. Our oldest daughter was conceived after 1.5 years of trying and fertility help. Our second daughter was conceived naturally, and we were so thankful to not have to do fertility treatments that time around. Unfortunately, she had trisomy 13 (a fatal condition), and we had to say hello and goodbye in one breath. Our family became complete when we had our son—*truly the rainbow after the storm.*

We've used the tactics outlined in this book with our two living children and have found great success. It quickly became a passion of mine, and I wanted to share with the world how my family is prioritizing sleep. And so, I am now a stay at home mom and author.

At the end of the day, the reality is you have to do what is best for you, your family, and your baby…and what worked great for one mom doesn't necessarily work great for another. There are certain things that I believe can work for everyone, though. This book is all of that—the stuff that can translate to all and really help everyone when it comes to the baby stages.

As an engineer we always said, "Don't reinvent the wheel," and "Share best practices." That's the idea of my writing…these are my best practices so that you might not have to reinvent!

I hope you've enjoyed the book. Best of luck to you in this amazing parenting adventure!

-Katrina

Index

N

O

P

R

S

T

U

W

Works Cited

Ezzo, G. (2012 5th Edition). On Becoming Babywise.

My Baby Sleep Guide. (n.d.). Retrieved from http://www.mybabysleepguide.com/2013/02/averag e-sleep-charts-by-age.html